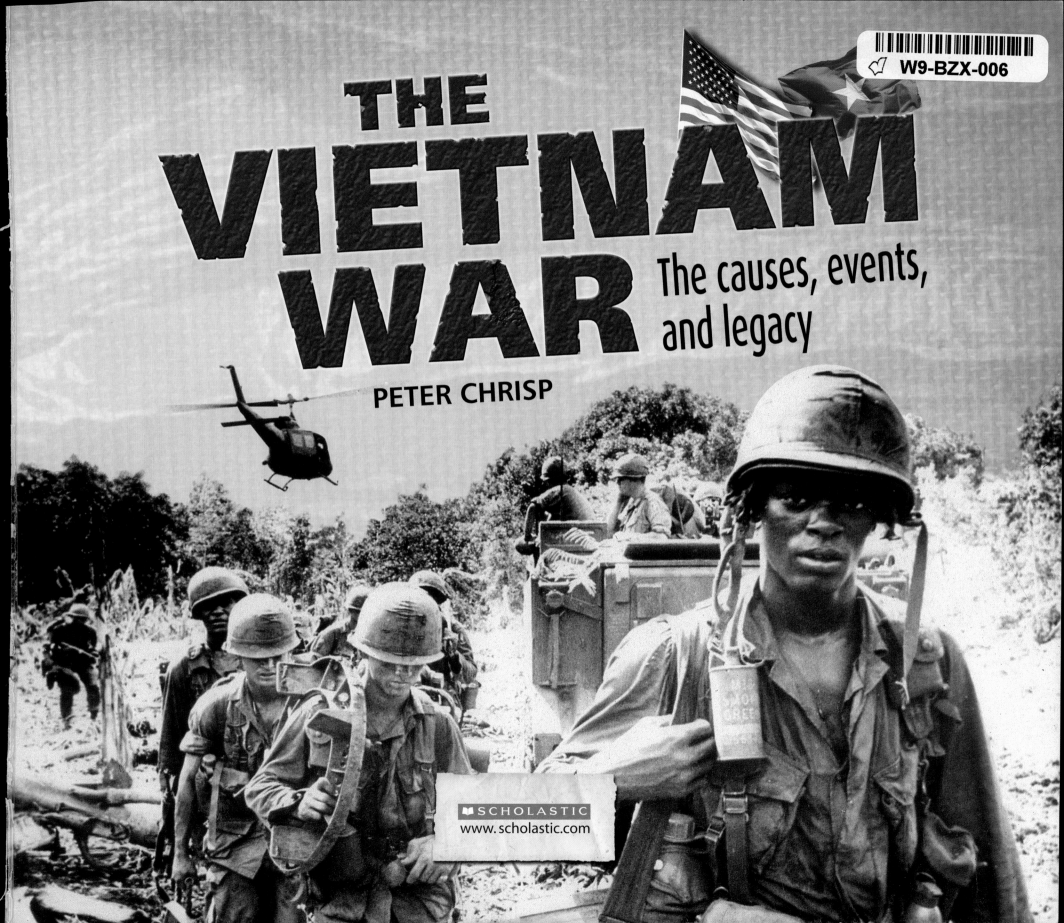

THE VIETNAM WAR

The causes, events, and legacy

PETER CHRISP

SCHOLASTIC
www.scholastic.com

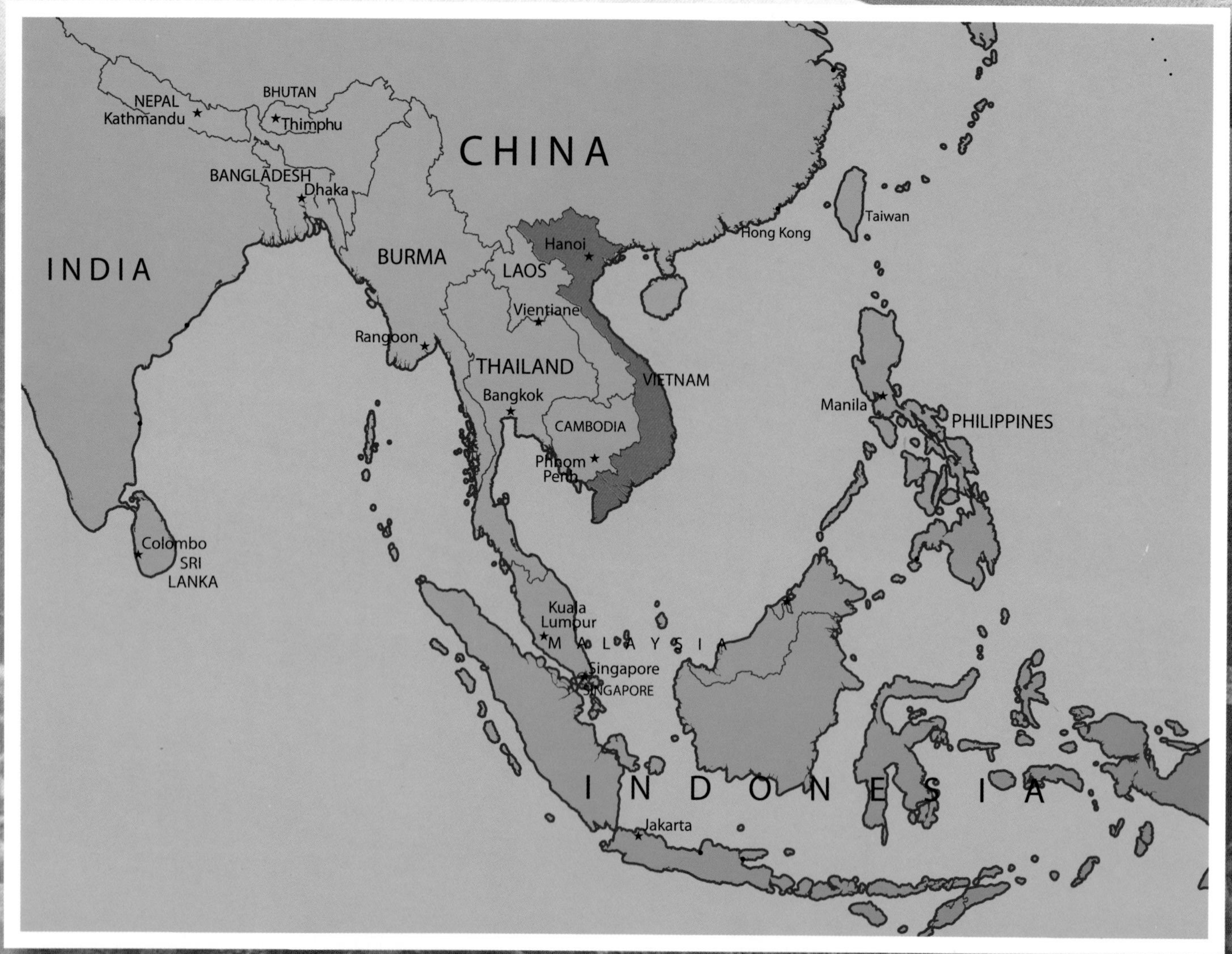

					CHINA				

NEPAL
Kathmandu ★

BHUTAN
★ Thimphu

BANGLADESH
★ Dhaka

INDIA

BURMA

LAOS

Hanoi

Hong Kong

Taiwan

Vientiane ★

Rangoon ★

THAILAND

Bangkok ★

VIETNAM

Manila ★

PHILIPPINES

CAMBODIA

Phnom ★
Penh

Colombo
SRI
LANKA

Kuala
Lumpur
★ M A L A Y S I A

Singapore
★ SINGAPORE

I N D O N E S I A

Jakarta ★

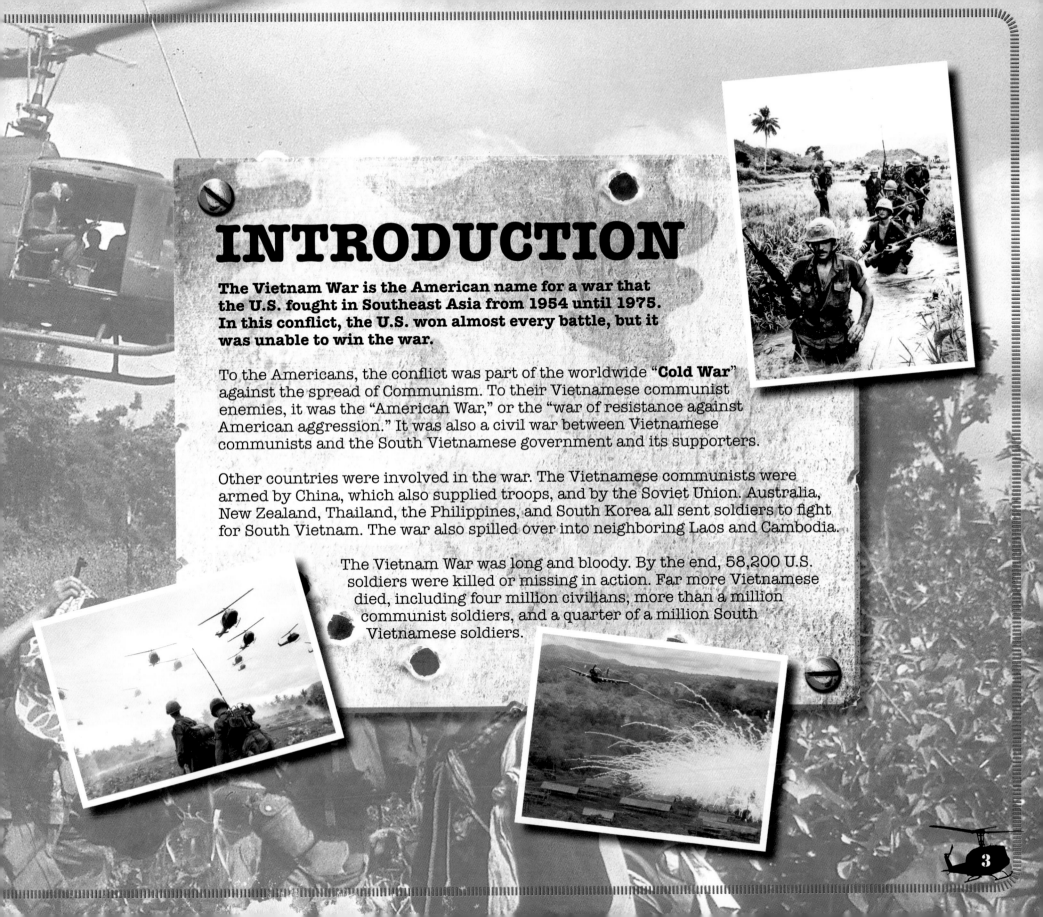

INTRODUCTION

The Vietnam War is the American name for a war that the U.S. fought in Southeast Asia from 1954 until 1975. In this conflict, the U.S. won almost every battle, but it was unable to win the war.

To the Americans, the conflict was part of the worldwide "**Cold War**" against the spread of Communism. To their Vietnamese communist enemies, it was the "American War," or the "war of resistance against American aggression." It was also a civil war between Vietnamese communists and the South Vietnamese government and its supporters.

Other countries were involved in the war. The Vietnamese communists were armed by China, which also supplied troops, and by the Soviet Union. Australia, New Zealand, Thailand, the Philippines, and South Korea all sent soldiers to fight for South Vietnam. The war also spilled over into neighboring Laos and Cambodia.

The Vietnam War was long and bloody. By the end, 58,200 U.S. soldiers were killed or missing in action. Far more Vietnamese died, including four million civilians, more than a million communist soldiers, and a quarter of a million South Vietnamese soldiers.

THE COLD WAR

The Cold War was waged by the world's most powerful nations, the U.S. and the Soviet Union, from 1945 until 1991. It is called the "Cold War" because there was no direct fighting between the superpowers. Each side had nuclear weapons, and so neither wanted to risk fighting a "Hot War."

CAPITALISM AND COMMUNISM

The U.S. was the world's richest capitalist country. Its society was based on individual liberty—the freedom of the individual to own capital (wealth), the freedom of the press, and the freedom to choose the government through multiparty elections. The Soviet Union was founded on the principle of equality. All property was owned by the state, only one political party was permitted, and the press was strictly censored. The aim was to create a society in which competition was replaced by government control.

DIVISIONS

The superpowers had been allies in World War II, but divisions quickly appeared between them. After the war's end, the Soviet Union imposed communism on the countries its armies occupied. Meanwhile, the U.S. supported anti-communist governments in Europe and Asia. So North Korea, which had been occupied by the Soviet Red Army, became a communist state. South Korea, backed by the U.S., remained capitalist.

THE TRUMAN DOCTRINE

On March 12, 1947, alarmed by the growth of Soviet power, U.S. President Harry S. Truman told **Congress** that it was the U.S.'s duty to help people who resist communism anywhere in the world. This idea, later called the **Truman Doctrine**, would guide U.S. foreign policy throughout the Cold War.

By 1949, communist nations stretched from East Germany to North Korea.

"At the present moment in world history nearly every nation must choose between alternative ways of life. The choice is too often not a free one."

President Harry S. Truman, Address to Congress, March 12, 1947

LOSING CHINA

In 1949, Mao Zedong's communists took control of China after winning a civil war. This was a big blow to U.S. prestige. President Truman, a Democrat, was accused by his Republican enemies of having "lost China."

Mao Zedong declaring the founding of the modern People's Republic of China, October 1, 1949

China's flag, adopted in 1949, was red for communism, with five golden stars, representing the unity of the people, led by the Communist Party.

KOREAN WAR

On June 25, 1950, communist North Korea launched a surprise invasion of South Korea. Led by the U.S., 21 member states of the United Nations sent troops to defend South Korea. The UN forces drove the communists back, and then invaded North Korea. The Chinese then intervened with a massive counterattack that saved the North. The Korean War dragged on until 1953.

This anti-communist **propaganda** poster shows "Communist Aggression," armed with a club, battering South Korea, which the United Nations rush to defend.

PRESIDENT EISENHOWER

In late 1952, Dwight D. Eisenhower, a popular retired U.S. general, was elected president. Eisenhower, a Republican, was an even tougher enemy of communism than Truman. Truman had talked only of "containing" communism, or stopping it from spreading; Eisenhower's administration promised to liberate countries under communist rule, a policy called "rollback."

In 1952, Eisenhower said,

"The French in Vietnam are fighting the same war we are in Korea."

THE DOMINO THEORY

In 1952, there was another war going on in Asia, in Vietnam. From 1946 Vietnamese nationalists, led by a communist, Ho Chi Minh, were fighting to drive out their French rulers. Eisenhower said that Vietnam must not fall to communism. He described Southeast Asia as a line of dominoes.

The domino theory meant that if one fell, it would knock over its neighbors. A communist Vietnam would threaten Laos, Cambodia, Thailand, Burma, Malaysia, and Indonesia.

VIETNAM

VIETNAMESE NATIONALISM

The country had a long tradition of resisting foreign rule, including a thousand-year struggle against the Chinese. From the beginning of the 20th century, Vietnamese **nationalists** called for an uprising against French rule.

Vietnam is a narrow, 1,240-mile-long country in Southeast Asia, with China to the north and Cambodia and Laos to the west. In 1887, it was part of French Indochina, which also included Cambodia and Laos.

CHINA

TONKIN

CHINA

Hanoi*

LAOS

*Luang Prabang

Gulf of Tonkin

Vientiane *

THAILAND

Hue *
Da Nang

* Pakse

ANNAM

Battambang *

CAMBODIA

Phnom Penh *

Saigon *
Cholon *
COCHINCHINA

Gulf of Thailand

French Indochina in 1899, with China to the north. Vietnam is split into three regions.

> "Frenchmen hold every lever of power; they hold the power of life and death over everyone. The life of thousands of Vietnamese people is not worth that of a French dog."
>
> Phan Boi Chau, Vietnamese nationalist, 1907

HO CHI MINH

Ho Chi Minh (1890–1969) spent much of his early life traveling the world. While in Paris, in 1920, he was converted to communism after reading about the Soviet leader, Lenin, who attacked **colonialism** (the rule of weak nations by richer, more powerful ones). Ho Chi Minh later wrote, "I wept for joy. Sitting by myself in my room, I would shout as if I were addressing large crowds:

> 'This is what we need, this is our path to liberation!'"

In 1930, in Hong Kong, Ho Chi Minh founded the Indochinese Communist Party.

WORLD WAR II

World War II brought the defeat of France by Germany in 1940, and the occupation of **Indochina**, by the Japanese in 1941. Seeing an opportunity to fight for independence, Ho Chi Minh returned to Vietnam and set up the **Viet Minh**, the "League for the Independence of Vietnam." This was a nationalist group that included many non-communists. Trained in **guerrilla** warfare by U.S. intelligence officers, the Viet Minh fought against the Japanese.

DECLARING INDEPENDENCE

On September 2, 1945, Japan surrendered to the U.S. and its allies. The same day, in Hanoi, Ho Chi Minh declared the independent Democratic Republic of Vietnam (**DRV**). Hoping to win U.S. backing, he quoted the 1776 U.S. Declaration of Independence:

> **"All men are created equal... with certain inalienable rights,... among these are Life, Liberty, and the Pursuit of Happiness."**

"ARE YOU A COMMUNIST?"

During the war, Ho Chi Minh had been able to hide his political beliefs from the Americans. But on September 15, 1945, just before leaving Vietnam, U.S. Major Allison Thomas asked him outright if he was a communist. Ho replied, "Yes. But we can still be friends, can't we?"

U.S. intelligence agents pose with the Viet Minh leadership in August 1945. Major Allison Thomas is the smiling figure next to Ho Chi Minh.

THE FRENCH RETURN

Three weeks after the declaration of independence, 80,000 French troops arrived in Saigon to re-establish their rule. The French easily took over southern Vietnam. Meanwhile, Ho Chi Minh, who remained in control in the north, tried to negotiate independence with the French government. Talks continued throughout much of 1946, but no agreement was reached.

Ho Chi Minh in France, 1946

French troops leave Marseilles for Indochina in 1945.

FIGHTING THE FRENCH

In November 1946, Ho Chi Minh's Viet Minh and the French went to war in Vietnam. While the French were able to hold the cities, the Viet Minh withdrew to the northern countryside, beginning an eight-year guerrilla war. From 1950, the Viet Minh were armed by China. The French war effort was paid for by the U.S., which also sent military advisers.

> "If we must fight, we will fight. You will kill ten of our men, and we will kill one of yours. Yet, in the end, it is you who will tire."
>
> Ho Chi Minh to the French in 1946

BAO DAI

The French claimed to rule Vietnam on behalf of Bao Dai (1913–97), the final emperor of the Nguyen Dynasty, established in 1825. Like all the emperors since 1889, Bao Dai was a figurehead with no real power.

Bao Dai, a playboy who spent most of his time in the south of France, had no interest in governing Vietnam.

VIÊT-NAM POSTES
BƯU CHÍNH
30$
5M BAO DAI

GENERAL VO NGUYEN GIAP

From 1944 to 1975, Vo Nguyen Giap (1911–2013), a former history teacher, was the leading Vietnamese communist general. He was a great strategist who understood how to defeat the French and the Americans. Unlike his enemies, Giap did not care how many soldiers he lost in his battles.

> "Every minute, hundreds of thousands of people die on this earth. The life or death of a hundred, a thousand, tens of thousands of human beings, even our compatriots, means little."
>
> Vo Nguyen Giap

DEFEATING THE FRENCH

The Viet Minh attack began on March 13, 1954, with a heavy bombardment that destroyed the French airfield. The French could not escape, or bring in supplies and reinforcements except by parachute. For two months, they faced constant bombardment and waves of charging Viet Minh soldiers. Finally, on May 7, 1954, the French surrendered. This was such a disastrous defeat that the French decided to pull out of Southeast Asia forever.

Giap, on the right, explains his plan to attack Dien Bien Phu. Ho Chi Minh is second left.

DIEN BIEN PHU

In late 1953, the French commander in chief, General Henri Navarre, set up a fortress, manned by 15,000 troops, in the valley of Dien Bien Phu in northwest Vietnam. Giap, seeing this as an opportunity to win a decisive victory, surrounded the fortress with 50,000 Viet Minh soldiers. He also used 200,000 peasant volunteers, who dragged heavy artillery pieces into the hills overlooking the French fortress.

Viet Minh soldiers have a victory parade through the streets of Hanoi in 1954.

French troops, trapped in Dien Bien Phu, anxiously await the next Viet Minh attack.

VIETNAM DIVIDED

Following the French surrender in Dien Bien Phu, an international conference in Geneva, Switzerland, decided on peace terms. Vietnam was temporarily divided into a communist state, north of the 17th parallel, and a non-communist south, under Emperor Bao Dai and his new prime minister, Ngo Din Diem. In 1956, there would be elections for a single Vietnamese government, when the country would be re-unified.

POPULATION MOVEMENT

Following the division of Vietnam, there was a mass movement of people between north and south. A million North Vietnamese moved south. Most were Catholics, landowners, and members of the middle classes who did not want to live under communism. At the same time 80,000 southerners, Viet Minh fighters and their families, moved north. Around 10,000 Viet Minh remained in the south, waiting for the election they believed would unite the country.

Refugees moving from North to South Vietnam board the *USS Montague* in the docks at Haiphong, part of "Operation Passage to Freedom."

Diem was declared president of the new southern Republic of Vietnam.

Vietnam was divided along the 17th parallel (the line of latitude 17 degrees north of the equator).

NGO DIN DIEM

Ngo Din Diem (1901–63) belonged to a wealthy Vietnamese Catholic family. He had a reputation as a tough anti-communist, but was also a nationalist who had opposed French rule. Diem distrusted Buddhists, who made up 80 percent of the population. He preferred to appoint fellow Catholics to positions of high authority.

PRESIDENT DIEM

In October 1955, Diem removed Bao Dai as head of state. Following a rigged **referendum**, in which he claimed 98.2 percent of the public had voted for him, Diem was declared president of the new Republic of South Vietnam. In July 1956, Diem announced that there would be no national elections. He knew that Ho Chi Minh would win and argued that there could not be a free election when there was a single-party state in the North. His aim was to make the division of Vietnam a lasting one.

In May 1957, Diem visited New York, where he was greeted by Eisenhower, who called him the "miracle man of Asia."

U.S. AID

In 1955, Eisenhower sent 700 military advisors to South Vietnam to train the **ARVN**, Diem's army. Over the next six years, Eisenhower also supplied billions of dollars in aid.

A U.S. military advisor trains a soldier of the new ARVN.

ARRESTS

Diem used his army to arrest suspected communists and other opponents. Between 1955–9, over 50,000 people were sent to prison camps and 12,000 were executed. Faced with the crackdown, the former Viet Minh fighters in the South took up arms against Diem's regime and appealed for help from the North.

The NLF flag, adopted in 1960

NATIONAL LIBERATION FRONT

In 1960, the southern resistance set up the National Liberation Front (**NLF**). Like the Viet Minh, it included non-communists, and did not mention socialism in its 1960 manifesto. This declared that the NLF's aim was "the realization of independence, democracy, peace, and neutrality pending the peaceful reunification of the fatherland." However, over time the northern communists took over the leadership of the NLF. Diem called the NLF the **"Viet Cong"** (Vietnamese communists).

Members of the NLF meet Ho Chi Minh in North Vietnam.

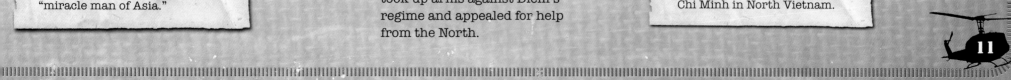

PRESIDENT KENNEDY'S WAR

In January 1961, John F. Kennedy became president of the United States. It was important for Kennedy, a young and inexperienced president, to appear to be a strong opponent of communism. He increased aid to South Vietnam. Under Kennedy the number of U.S. advisors grew from 685 to 16,700. Despite this assistance, the situation in South Vietnam worsened due to the misrule of President Diem.

Peasants hated being made to move into strategic hamlets, which took them away from their traditional homes and farming grounds.

STRATEGIC HAMLETS

Diem tried to separate the peasants from the Viet Cong by resettling them in fortified villages called **strategic hamlets**. The peasants, supplied with weapons, were expected to defend themselves. The program was run by a secret communist agent, Pham Ngoc Thao, who made sure it failed. Thao placed the villages in remote places with a strong Viet Cong presence. The Viet Cong confiscated thousands of weapons from the peasants, who saw no reason why they should fight. One peasant said, "Why should we die for weapons?"

Kennedy was the second-youngest U.S. president. He was 43 years old when he took office.

THE BUDDHIST CRISIS

Diem also persecuted Buddhists. In 1963, after he banned the display of religious flags on the Buddha's birthday, 10,000 people demonstrated in protest. Diem's soldiers fired into the crowds, killing nine people and wounding many others. In protest, a 73-year-old Buddhist monk, Thich Quang Duc, burned himself to death in front of a U.S. news photographer.

Buddhist monks and women pull at a barbed wire road barricade in front of the Giac Minh pagoda in 1963.

The photograph of Thich Quang Duc burning himself to death was printed all around the world.

ATTACK ON THE PAGODAS

President Kennedy tried to persuade Diem to fire his brother and end his anti-Buddhist policies. Instead, in August 1963, Diem allowed Nhu to launch an attack on Buddhist pagodas (temples), arresting thousands of Buddhists.

MR. AND MRS. NHU

Much of the blame for the attack on Buddhists lay with Diem's brother and chief advisor, Ngo Dinh Nhu, who was head of the secret police. The situation was made worse by Nhu's outspoken and bloodthirsty wife, Madame Nhu. She told journalists that she had clapped her hands with glee when she heard of the monk's suicide, and offered a box of matches for the "next barbecue."

Madame Nhu was nicknamed the "dragon lady of Vietnam" by U.S. journalists.

COUP AGAINST DIEM

Diem had by now lost so much support that a group of South Vietnamese generals plotted to overthrow him. They asked the U.S. ambassador how Kennedy would react to this plan. Kennedy reluctantly gave his backing. On November 2, the generals arrested Diem and his brother Nhu, and murdered them both. When Kennedy heard the news, he turned pale with shock.

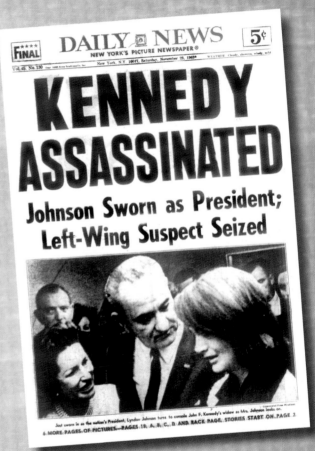

FINAL **DAILY NEWS** **5¢**
NEW YORK'S PICTURE NEWSPAPER®

KENNEDY ASSASSINATED

Johnson Sworn as President; Left-Wing Suspect Seized

KENNEDY ASSASSINATED

Just three weeks after Diem's murder, Kennedy himself was shot by an assassin in Dallas, Texas. One great question of the Vietnam War is: What would Kennedy have done if he had lived? Several of his aides believed that he was planning to withdraw from Vietnam in 1964. But others, including Vice President Lyndon Johnson, thought he would stop at nothing to win the war.

PRESIDENT JOHNSON

The new president, Lyndon Baines Johnson, inherited a worsening situation in Vietnam. The generals who overthrew Diem were unable to provide strong leadership and soon fell from power, only to be replaced by other ineffective generals. Meanwhile, the Viet Cong were increasing their control over the countryside. From 1964 they were joined by well-trained units of the North Vietnamese Army (NVA).

Johnson and Robert McNamara in a meeting about Vietnam in 1965

ADVISORS

Johnson had the same military advisors as Kennedy, including Robert McNamara, Secretary of Defense; McGeorge Bundy, National Security Advisor; Dean Rusk, Secretary of State; and General Maxwell Taylor, ambassador to South Vietnam. They persuaded him that the U.S. urgently needed to increase financial and military aid to the South to prevent the regime from collapsing.

Just two hours after Kennedy's assassination, Johnson takes the oath of office onboard Air Force One. Kennedy's stunned widow, Jackie, stands beside him.

"Tell those generals in Saigon... I want them to get off their butts and get out in those jungles and whip hell out of some communists. And then I want them to leave me alone, because I got some bigger things to do at home."

Lyndon Johnson to his advisors, November 23, 1963

LYNDON JOHNSON

As president, Lyndon Johnson's central aim was to build a "Great Society," which involved giving equal **civil rights** to black Americans and improving education, health care, and housing provision for the poor. He did not want to fight a war in Southeast Asia, but he felt that he could not afford to be seen as the president who lost Vietnam.

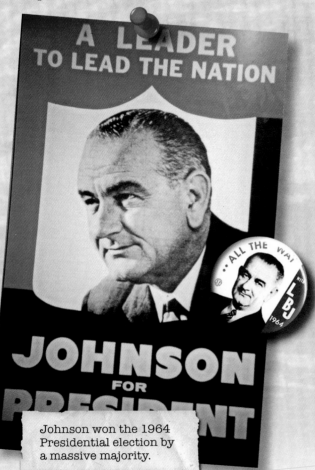

Johnson won the 1964 Presidential election by a massive majority.

"**We are not about to send American boys nine or ten thousand miles away from home to do what Asian boys ought to be doing for themselves.**"

Lyndon Johnson, campaigning to be elected president, October 21, 1964

USS Constellation in the Gulf of Tonkin in 1964

THE TONKIN RESOLUTION

In August 1964, two U.S. Naval destroyers reported attacks by North Vietnamese patrol boats in the Gulf of Tonkin. Johnson used the incident to get Congress to pass a resolution allowing him "to take all necessary measures" in the defense of South Vietnam. The Tonkin Resolution was passed by an overwhelming majority, with only two senators voting against it. This gave Johnson the legal power to wage war against North Vietnam.

ROLLING THUNDER

The North Vietnamese saw the Tonkin Resolution as a U.S. declaration of war, and began to attack U.S. bases in South Vietnam. In February 1965, following an attack on an American airfield at Pleiku, McGeorge Bundy persuaded Johnson to respond with large-scale bombing of the North. The bombing campaign, later called "**Rolling Thunder**," was limited to military targets such as railways, power plants, and oil depots. Populated regions and areas close to the Chinese border were not hit.

NORTH VIETNAMESE DEFENSES

The North Vietnamese defended themselves using Chinese and Soviet fighter planes, Chinese anti-aircraft guns, and surface-to-air guided missiles, operated by Chinese troops. During the whole three-year bombing campaign, the U.S. would lose 938 aircraft, with 1,084 airmen killed, captured, or missing.

The campaign used the new U.S. Navy A-6 Intruder, which combined long-range, accurate bombing and an ability to fly in all weather conditions and at night.

THE GROUND WAR

Bombing the North had little effect on the communist campaign in South Vietnam, and it also led to a change in the war on the ground. General Westmoreland, fearing that the communists would attack the air bases used by the bombers, persuaded Johnson to send in U.S. soldiers to guard them.

THE FIRST GROUND TROOPS

On March 8, 1965, the first ground troops, two battalions of Marines, landed at Danang. They were followed in April by 40,000 additional troops. The soldiers' purpose was seen as purely defensive. They would protect U.S. bases and civilian areas while offensive operations were left to the ARVN (Army of the Republic of Vietnam). This was called the "enclave strategy."

GENERAL WESTMORELAND

General William Westmoreland (1914–2005) was the U.S. commander in Vietnam from 1964–8. He believed that the way to win was to kill so many communist troops that North Vietnam would finally reach a "crossover point" and lose the will to continue the war. This is called a strategy of **attrition** (gradual wearing down).

General Westmoreland was confident that he could beat the NVA and Viet Cong.

ON THE OFFENSIVE

General Westmoreland was against the enclave strategy from the start. The ARVN was unable to beat the better-trained NVA in battle. He felt that his much more effective American troops were wasted defending bases. Westmoreland urged Johnson to let him go on the offensive, and take the war to the enemy. In June 1965, after further ARVN defeats, Johnson agreed.

A young U.S. Marine, photographed after arriving in Danang

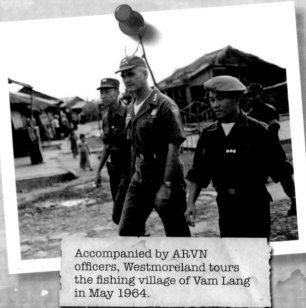

Accompanied by ARVN officers, Westmoreland tours the fishing village of Vam Lang in May 1964.

AN AMERICAN WAR

As the Americans began their offensives, the ARVN was sidelined. The South Vietnamese soldiers, who were badly led, poorly paid, and had inferior weapons, came to believe that the main fighting could be left to the Americans. They felt that it had become an American war.

Johnson and Westmoreland with the South Vietnamese leaders, President Nguyen Van Thieu (third from right) and Prime Minister Nguyen Cao Ky (right)

"**They transformed the Vietnam War into a conflict between the United States and North Vietnam ... The government of South Vietnam ... became, in the eyes of the people and of the world, a puppet regime serving the interests of American imperialists.**"

Lt. General Nguyen Cao Ky, Prime Minister of South Vietnam from 1965–7

U.S. MARINE

On patrol, marines were heavily laden with equipment, which slowed them down as they moved through swamps and jungle.

Steel Helmet
M1 steel helmet, with a camouflaged cloth cover, forest green on one side and brown on the other. In Vietnam, it was worn green side out.

Pack
Loaded with signal flares, smoke grenades, dry socks, a poncho, and three days' rations. On the back, there would be an entrenching tool.

Hand Grenades
Carried on the flak jacket, the M67 was a fragmentation grenade that exploded as a deadly shower of steel fragments.

Flak Jacket
The flak jacket, made of strong fiberglass plates sewn into nylon, was a type of body armor. It weighed 10 pounds.

Uniform
Green cotton fatigue shirt and pants. The cargo pockets might hold a map, compass, halazone water purification pills, insect repellent, malaria tablets, cigarettes, and chewing gum.

M14 Rifle
The M14 rifle, the main U.S. infantry weapon used until 1967, could fire 750 rounds a minute.

Belt
Holding two water canteens, ammunition, and a machete, with an 18-inch steel blade, for hacking through thick vegetation.

COMMUNIST FORCES

A Viet Cong propaganda poster

The Americans had to fight two armies in South Vietnam. There was the South Vietnamese **PLAF** (People's Liberation Armed Forces), better known as the Viet Cong (Vietnamese communists). There was also the regular army of North Vietnam, the **PAVN** (People's Army of North Vietnam), which the Americans called the **NVA**. Although the communists pretended that the PLAF was an independent freedom movement, it took all its orders from the North.

TRAINING

Many of the first Viet Cong were former South Vietnamese Viet Minh fighters who had moved north in 1956. In the North, they received military and political training, learning how to use guns, build booby traps, and set ambushes. After returning south along the **Ho Chi Minh Trail**, they set about recruiting more fighters from the peasantry.

PART-TIME FIGHTERS

The Viet Cong included full-time soldiers, known as the **Main Force**, and part-time soldiers who lived as farmers by day and fighters at night. Both men and women fought in the Viet Cong, which made it almost impossible for Americans to tell combatants from civilians.

This cross-section shows one of the communists' many secret underground bases.

THE TUNNEL NETWORK

The full-time Viet Cong hid in the daytime in a network of tunnels, which the communists had been digging since the war against the French in concrete-like soil. The biggest, at Cu Chi, comprised 155 miles of tunnels, and included meeting halls and hospitals. Tunnel entrances were too narrow for most Americans to squeeze through, but they were also protected by booby-trapped pits. Entrances were so well hidden that one U.S. division built its camp right on top of a tunnel network!

A female Viet Cong fighter

A VIET CONG FIGHTER

Viet Cong fighters were much more lightly equipped than the Americans. This made it easy for them to move quickly through forests, and also to blend in with the civilian population. They could live for days on a small amount of rice, flavored with fish paste.

B-40 grenade launcher
Fired from the shoulder

Cotton bush hat
Fighters also wore pith helmets with camouflaged covers

Dried rice
Kept in a linen tube worn over the shoulder

Shoulder bags
For carrying ammunition

AK-47 assault rifle
Chinese or Russian, could fire 600 rounds per minute

Uniform
Black cotton pajama-style trousers and top

"Uncle Ho" sandals
With soles made from old tires

THE NVA

The North Vietnamese Army troops, recruited in the North, went through eight months of military and political training. They were dedicated and highly disciplined. In South Vietnam, to avoid U.S. forces, they were constantly on the move from one fortified camp to another.

Pith helmet
With green cloth cover

Pouches
For ammunition and equipment

AK-47 assault rifle
Chinese or Russian, could fire 600 rounds per minute

Uniform
Olive green shirt and trousers

Rubber shoes

AN NVA FIGHTER

Because they often had to live in the forest, NVA fighters needed more supplies than the Viet Cong. Each man carried a canvas bag, hammock, mosquito net, raincoat, canteen, halazone pills, vitamin pills, quinine (anti-malaria pills), and bags of dried rice.

SEARCH AND DESTROY

General Westmoreland believed that the way to win the war was not to try to seize territory, but to seek out enemy forces and kill as many of them as possible. **"Search and destroy,"** as it was called, depended on new airmobile tactics. With the 435 helicopters of the 1st Cavalry Division, Westmoreland could land troops in combat anywhere in South Vietnam.

American troops at Plei Mei

PLEI MEI

In late 1965, General Giap was as eager as Westmoreland to fight a battle. While Westmoreland wanted to try his new airmobile tactics, Giap needed to learn about the strengths and weaknesses of the U.S. enemy. On October 19, Giap sent a large NVA force of two regiments to attack the U.S. **special forces** camp at Plei Mei. After fierce fighting, the attackers, driven back by U.S. bomber planes, withdrew west to hills overlooking the Ia Drang Valley.

"What kind of fighters are the Viet Cong that you met here?"

"I would give anything to have two hundred of them under my command. They're the finest soldiers I've ever seen."

CBS television news interview with Major Charles Beckwith, after the battle of Plei Mei, October 1965

American men of the 1st Cavalry Division move toward their helicopters as they prepare for a search and destroy mission.

Taking cover from fire at Plei Mei

THE BATTLE OF IA DRANG VALLEY

On November 14, Westmoreland's helicopters found the NVA at Ia Drang and landed the first troops, who quickly realized they were outnumbered. As the battle raged, the U.S. sent in B-52 bomber planes, fighter-bombers, and helicopters with reinforcements. It was the bloodiest battle yet, and by the end, on November 26, 305 Americans and 3,561 NVA troops had been killed.

"HANGING ONTO THE AMERICANS' BELT"

At Ia Drang, U.S. planes attacked the Vietnamese with bombs filled with **napalm**, jellied petroleum that stuck to anything it touched, burning fiercely. To avoid napalm, the Vietnamese learned to fight at close quarters. This required great discipline. It meant they had to wait until U.S. troops were on top of them before opening fire. They called this tactic "**hanging onto the Americans' belt**."

Napalm bombs explode in fields south of Saigon.

Major Bruce Crandall flew his helicopter 22 times into the battlefield, bringing supplies and ammunition and evacuating the wounded.

DIFFERENT LESSONS

Each side learned different lessons from the battle at Ia Drang. Westmoreland believed that the massive NVA losses showed that his attrition strategy was correct. Giap learned to avoid set battles. In future, the communists would decide when and where to fight before retreating over the border into neutral Laos and Cambodia.

The second wave of combat helicopters of the 1st Air Cavalry Division fly over U.S. troops during Operation Pershing, a search and destroy mission on the Bong Son Plain and An Lao Valley of South Vietnam.

SEARCHING THE VILLAGES

To find the Viet Cong, U.S. troops would descend on a village and sweep through it, searching for weapons and concealed tunnels, and interrogating villagers. The Viet Cong were expert at hiding, crawling into tunnels or under buildings and rubbish heaps. In river areas, they would hide underwater, breathing through bamboo tubes.

CLEARING A TUNNEL

On discovering the entrance to a tunnel, soldiers would often throw grenades with tear gas or white phosphorus inside. The phosphorus grenades produced a cloud of hot, dense smoke that would kill anybody caught underground. There were also volunteers, nicknamed "tunnel rats," who would search the tunnels with a flashlight and pistol.

AMBUSHES

On patrol, U.S. troops could never feel safe. The Viet Cong were skilled at laying ambushes. At any moment, the Americans might be blown up by a booby trap or shot by a sniper. This encouraged them to distrust the peasants. They had no way of telling who was Viet Cong.

A U.S. soldier prepares to throw a grenade into a tunnel.

Viet Cong fighters hiding in a lotus field

A 17-year-old boy weeps beside the body of his mother, executed by the Viet Cong.

PEOPLE'S COURTS

The peasants also had to worry about the Viet Cong, who would return after the U.S. troops left, arresting anybody accused of informing. They held "people's courts" in the villages where suspected informers were tried and executed, or sent to prison camps.

"We found most people didn't even know the difference between communism and democracy. They only wanted to work in rice paddies without helicopters strafing them and bombs with napalm burning their villages and tearing their country apart."

John Kerry, a veteran who became an opponent of the war, 1971.

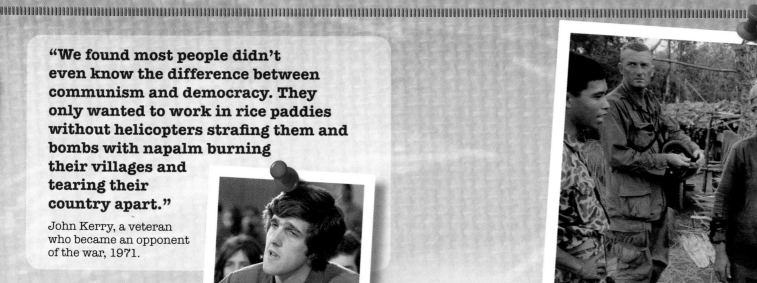

A soldier questions a woman in Phu Cat village.

KILLING CIVILIANS

"Search and destroy" left the Viet Cong and NVA in control of the countryside. American troops would find themselves fighting again and again in the same places. This made it difficult for the U.S. public to see if the war was being won. The tactic, which measured success by the numbers of dead, encouraged the killing of civilians. It also created many refugees.

"Our mission was not to win terrain or seize positions, but simply ... to kill communists and to kill as many of them as possible ... The pressure ... to produce enemy corpses was intense ... This led to such practices as counting civilians as Viet Cong. 'If it's dead and Vietnamese, it's VC,' was a rule of thumb in the bush."

Marine Lt. Philip Caputo

Terrified villagers cower as U.S. troops storm their village, searching for the Viet Cong.

THE HO CHI MINH TRAIL

The North responded to search and destroy by sending more NVA units down the Ho Chi Minh Trail, the supply route that passed from North to South Vietnam through Laos and Cambodia. It took from two to six months to complete the whole journey. Over time, the trail network grew until it included 10,000 miles of roads.

BUILDING THE TRAIL

The trail was built and maintained by the NVA's Logistics Group 559, which included 100,000 men and women who continuously expanded and improved it. Over time, the routes of the trail multiplied, and it came to include an oil pipeline, anti-aircraft units, and underground hospitals and barracks. There was even a troupe of actors who staged political plays to motivate the soldiers.

This cave on the trail has been converted into a vehicle-repair shop.

Bicycles, heavily loaded with supplies, are wheeled along the trail. Ong Phung Minh, who helped build the trail, later recalled, "The route had to be passable for bicycles. Bicycles were our secret weapon."

Elephants were also used to carry supplies along the trail.

THE SIHANOUK TRAIL

In Cambodia, the communists were able to bring in Chinese military supplies by sea, through the port of Sihanoukville. Prince Sihanouk, ruler of Cambodia, made a deal with the North Vietnamese, allowing them to use the port. The Americans called the route across Cambodia the "Sihanouk Trail."

This map shows the routes of the Ho Chi Minh Trail and the Sihanouk Trail.

"I have traveled down the trail many times, beginning with my first trip, when I transported material in a bamboo basket strapped to my back. On my next trip, I graduated to carrying supplies by bicycle. Finally I traveled down the trail with mechanized transport divisions."

Colonel Bui Tin of the NVA

These NVA troops, marching along the trail, use a wooden ladder to climb a steep hill.

In 1966, NVA soldiers, carrying greenery for camouflage, move across an open stretch of the trail. In later years, most of the route would be covered.

BOMBING THE TRAIL

President Johnson could not openly attack the trail, because Laos and Cambodia were neutral countries. However, in December 1964, after winning the backing of the Laotian prime minister, Johnson approved a secret bombing campaign of the trail in Laos, called Operation Barrel Roll. The North Vietnamese could not complain because the trail itself was a violation of Laotian neutrality. Both sides kept this part of the war a secret from the outside world. Bombing was difficult because much of the trail, hidden by a thick canopy of trees, could not be seen from the air. The North Vietnamese also built dummy trails to draw attack from the U.S. bombers.

THE ANTIWAR MOVEMENT

From 1964, there was a growing antiwar movement in the United States. It began in the universities with "teach-ins" (antiwar lectures and debates). Opposition came from many different groups, including students, campaigners for black civil rights, members of the hippie "counter-culture," churches, and Vietnam veterans. Although the antiwar movement received great publicity, polls showed that most Americans continued to support the war as long as victory seemed likely. Patriotic conservative Americans were disgusted to see people waving the North Vietnamese flag at demonstrations.

DRAFT RESISTERS

Opposition to the war was fueled by the draft, the calling up of young men into the armed forces. Thousands of Americans refused to serve, burning their draft cards in protest. The most famous draft resister was heavyweight boxing champion Muhammad Ali, who was stripped of his title as a result.

FLOWER POWER

In 1965, the poet Allen Ginsberg suggested that antiwar protesters carry flowers to give out to policemen and onlookers. He described this as a form of street theater, reducing the likelihood of violence.

Protesters place flowers in the barrels of National Guardsmen's rifles during a 1965 demonstration in Washington.

VIETNAM VETERANS AGAINST THE WAR

The most powerful opposition came from Vietnam Veterans Against the War. This group was founded in 1967 by former soldiers who had fought in Vietnam and now viewed the war as wrong. They held meetings and protest marches, where many threw away the medals they had won. By 1971, VVAW had around 11,000 members.

Vietnam veterans march against the war in Miami in 1972. One disabled veteran protests by flying the U.S. flag upside-down.

MARTIN LUTHER KING

Dr. Martin Luther King, the black civil rights leader, made many anti-war speeches. In April 1967, he accused the government of "taking the young black men who had been crippled by our society and sending them 8,000 miles away to guarantee liberties in Southeast Asia which they had not found in Southwest Georgia and East Harlem."

Heavily armed National Guardsmen face student demonstrators at Kent State University in May 1970.

VIOLENT CLASHES

As the war continued, protests were marked with increased violence from demonstrators and police. In May 1970, confronted by rock-throwing demonstrators at Kent State University, **National Guardsmen** opened fire on the crowd, killing four students and wounding nine others.

HANOI JANE

One of the most outspoken opponents of the war was the movie star Jane Fonda. In 1972, Fonda visited Hanoi, making speeches denouncing U.S. soldiers in Vietnam as war criminals. Many Americans saw her as a traitor, and nicknamed her "Hanoi Jane."

In Hanoi, Jane Fonda, sitting on an anti-aircraft gun, sings an antiwar song surrounded by reporters and soldiers.

"Every day our leadership would listen to world news ... to follow the growth of the American antiwar movement. Visits to Hanoi by people like Jane Fonda ... gave us confidence that we should hold on in the face of battlefield reverses."

Colonel Bui Tin of the NVA, interviewed in 1995

THE TET OFFENSIVE

In January 1968, during the festival of Tet, the Viet Cong and NVA launched a massive attack on the cities and towns of South Vietnam. Called the **Tet Offensive**, it took the U.S. and South Vietnamese armies completely by surprise.

GENERAL GIAP'S PLAN

General Giap, the northern commander, spent months preparing for the offensive, sending NVA troops and supplies south. Meanwhile, the Viet Cong, dressed as civilians, moved from the countryside into the cities, smuggling in thousands of weapons. The communists hoped that a big offensive would set off a mass uprising and topple the southern government.

Because his forces were still greatly outnumbered, Giap planned to stage the offensive during Tet, the most important Vietnamese festival. During Tet, a celebration of the New Year and family ancestors, it was usual for both sides to declare a truce, so that soldiers could celebrate with their families. As a result of the truce, half of the South Vietnamese army would be on leave.

General Vo Nguyen Giap of the NVA

KHE SANH

To lure U.S. troops away from the cities before the offensive, the NVA mounted a series of attacks on remote outposts. The biggest took place on January 21 at Khe Sanh in the northwest, where 17,200 NVA troops surrounded 6,000 U.S. marines. General Westmoreland rushed U.S. reinforcements to Khe Sanh, and the longest and bloodiest battle of the war began.

A U.S. tank races to Khe Sanh, to help outnumbered American forces.

An ammunition bunker explodes in front of U.S. Marines in Khe Sanh.

A marine in Khe Sanh wrote a quotation from *Newsweek* magazine on his jacket.

"CAUTION: BEING A MARINE IN KHE SANH MAY BE HAZARDOUS TO YOUR HEALTH." 3ᵈ BN. 26ᵗʰ "NEWSWEEK"

ATTACK ON THE CITIES

The Tet Offensive began in the early hours of January 31, when 84,000 Viet Cong and NVA soldiers attacked 100 cities and towns across the south. In Saigon, 19 Viet Cong fighters even blasted their way into the U.S. Embassy compound, though all were killed in the following gun battle.

Although taken by surprise, the U.S. and South Vietnamese armies reacted quickly, and in most places, defeated the attackers in a few days. There was no civilian uprising. In Saigon, the city was cleared after two weeks of street fighting.

Following the fighting, the Cholon district of Saigon was destroyed.

The communists attacked cities and towns through-out South Vietnam.

BOTH SIDES LOST

The Tet Offensive was a military defeat for the communists, who lost almost 60,000 troops, including the best Viet Cong fighters. From now on, the NVA would be the main fighting force on the communist side. In the United States, however, the outcome was not seen as a victory. Just a few months before, the public had been reassured by General Westmoreland that the war was almost won. The massive size of the Tet Offensive came as a huge shock, shaking support for the war. As reports of the fighting first came in on the television news, leading U.S. newscaster Walter Cronkite exclaimed,

"What the hell is going on?! I thought we were winning the war!"

BATTLE OF HUE

The fiercest fighting took place in Hue, the former capital, where the NVA seized control of the strongly defended old city and held out for almost a month. While in control of Hue, the communists killed 3,000 civilians who were seen as supporters of the southern government. At the end of the battle, the city lay in ruins.

These U.S. Marines in Hue are shooting at communist snipers near the old citadel.

Walter Cronkite delivers the evening news.

STALEMATE

On March 31, 1968, President Johnson made a television speech from the White House in which he said, "I am taking the first step to de-escalate the conflict." He would not stand for re-election, but would devote his remaining time in office to finding peace. To get Hanoi to negotiate, Johnson called a halt to the bombing campaign of North Vietnam.

Following the Tet Offensive, on February 27, 1968, CBS newscaster Walter Cronkite made a television broadcast in which he announced, "It seems now more certain than ever that the bloody experience of Vietnam is to end in a **stalemate**." Watching the broadcast, President Johnson said to an aide, "If I've lost Cronkite, I've lost Middle America."

WESTMORELAND REPLACED

General Westmoreland believed that the failure of the Tet Offensive gave him the ideal opportunity to win the war. All he needed, he said, was 206,000 more troops. President Johnson, who had already sent 500,000 American soldiers to Vietnam, did not agree. He was so shaken by Tet that he refused the general's request and brought him back to America to be Chief of Staff. Westmoreland argued in later years that he had been cheated of victory.

> "It was like two boxers in the ring, one having the other on the ropes, close to a knock-out, when the apparent winner's second inexplicably throws in the towel."
>
> General Westmoreland,
> *A Soldier Reports*, 1976

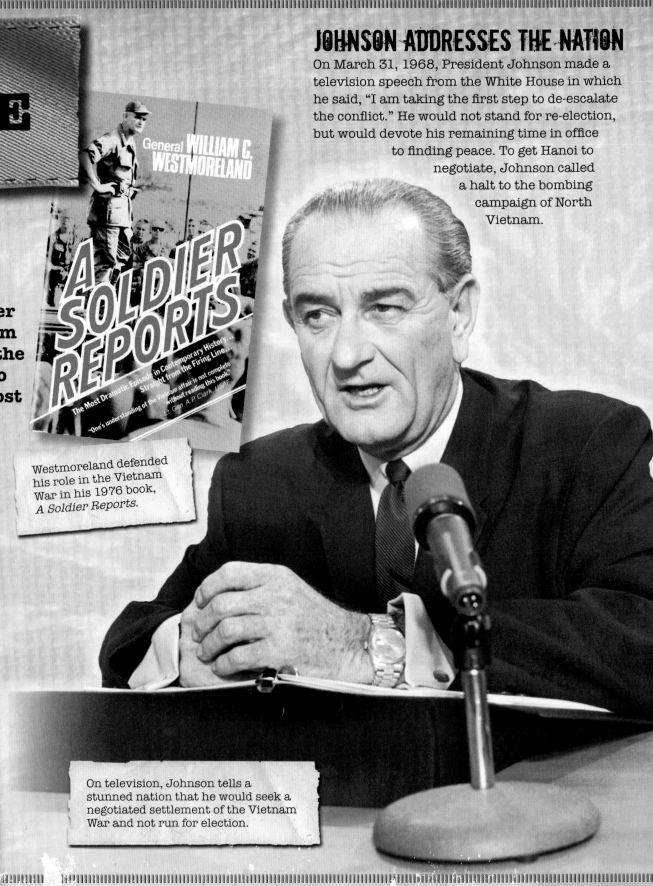

General WILLIAM C. WESTMORELAND

A SOLDIER REPORTS

The Most Dramatic Episode in Contemporary History... Straight from the Firing Line...

"One's understanding of the Vietnam affair is not complete without reading this book."
— Lt. Gen. A. P. Clark, USAF

Westmoreland defended his role in the Vietnam War in his 1976 book, *A Soldier Reports*.

On television, Johnson tells a stunned nation that he would seek a negotiated settlement of the Vietnam War and not run for election.

LOSS OF MORALE

The realization that there would now be no final victory damaged U.S. military morale, or fighting spirit. Soldiers saw no sense in risking their lives for an unwinnable war. Many soldiers decorated their equipment with peace signs and antiwar slogans, such as "We are the unwilling, led by the unqualified, doing the unnecessary, for the ungrateful."

This U.S. soldier has written the word "peace" on his camouflaged cloth helmet cover.

FRAGGING

U.S. officers who ordered men on dangerous missions now ran the risk of being "fragged"— killed by their own men using fragmentation grenades. The army reported 1,016 **fragging** cases between 1969 and 1972, resulting in 86 deaths and over 700 injuries.

Vietnamese peasants from My Lai village

MY LAI

U.S. soldiers often took out their anger and frustration on Vietnamese civilians. The most shocking case was the March 1968 massacre of between 347 and 504 old men, women, and children in the village of My Lai. The army attempted to cover up the massacre, but it was revealed by the press in November 1969. One of the soldiers, Paul Meadlo, described the killings in a newspaper interview. His mother, sitting beside him, said, "I sent them a good boy and they turned him into a murderer."

After the My Lai massacre, U.S. soldiers burned the whole village to the ground.

"If somebody gives you orders that would kill you and your squad ... then you eliminate them, 'cause that's the only way you'll get another officer. And, it's better that one of them goes instead of all of you."

George Cantero, U.S. Army medic

VIETNAMIZATION

General Creighton Abrams, who replaced Westmoreland as U.S. commander in Vietnam in 1968, had very different ideas about how to fight the war. He called a halt to Westmoreland's large-scale search and destroy missions. Abrams' aim was to "clear and hold" the countryside, providing security for the population. He used small patrols whose role was to cut the Viet Cong and NVA off from the people.

U.S. and ARVN troops leap from a helicopter as they prepare to move into a combat area.

General Creighton Abrams (1914-1974) brought new energy to the conduct of the war.

ARMING THE ARVN

Abrams built up the ARVN, which was given modern weapons and used more often in combined missions with the U.S. military. He stressed a policy later called the **"Vietnamization"** of the war.

With their American manufactured arms and uniforms, ARVN soldiers looked a lot like U.S. soldiers. This helped the communists portray the ARVN as "puppets" of the Americans.

PRESIDENT NIXON

On November 5, 1968, the Republican Richard Nixon was elected president. During the election, Nixon hinted he had a secret plan to end the war and said he would bring "peace with honor." This meant preserving the South Vietnamese government without the support of U.S. troops. The difficulty of achieving this goal led to four more years of warfare.

FOR EXPERIENCED LEADERSHIP
19 68
NIXON FOR PRESIDENT

REDUCING U.S. TROOP LEVELS

In 1969, Nixon announced the first reductions in U.S. troop levels—25,000 in June followed by 60,000 in December. At the same time, he increased funding for the ARVN, which grew in size from 427,000 men, in 1968, to 516,000 in 1971.

> **"We linked the pace of our withdrawal to the progress of Vietnamization ... As South Vietnamese forces became stronger, the rate of American withdrawal could become stronger."**
>
> Richard Nixon, *No More Vietnams*, 1985

HAMBURGER HILL

In May 1969, U.S. and South Vietnamese forces attacked an NVA base on Ap Bia Mountain, near the border with Laos. There was a fierce ten-day battle. U.S. casualties were 72 dead and 372 wounded. The soldiers nicknamed the battlefield "Hamburger Hill," because they felt that they had been thrown into a meat grinder. After the battle, a soldier nailed a sign saying "Hamburger Hill" to a charred tree stump. Beneath, another soldier wrote, "Was it worth it?"

U.S. paratroopers rest at the top of Ap Bia Mountain.

33

WIDENING THE WAR

In February 1969, two months after becoming president, Nixon widened the war by ordering the bombing of Cambodia, to hit the NVA system of base camps. Since Cambodia was a neutral country, Nixon kept the bombing secret from Congress and American journalists.

Cambodia was heavily bombed by U.S. B-52 planes from 1969 until 1973.

PRINCE SIHANOUK OVERTHROWN

Prince Sihanouk, the leftist Cambodian ruler, had kept his country out of the war by tolerating the presence of the Vietnamese bases. However, in March 1970, Sihanouk was overthrown by Lon Nol, an anti-communist general. Lon Nol then ordered the North Vietnamese to leave Cambodia. The North Vietnamese joined forces with the **Khmer Rouge**, the Cambodian communists, and launched an offensive against Lon Nol's government.

In 1970, Lon Nol made himself president of the Khmer Republic, which lasted until 1975, when he was overthrown by the Khmer Rouge.

After his overthrow, Prince Sihanouk allied himself with the Khmer Rouge and the Vietnamese Communists.

INVADING CAMBODIA

To save Lon Nol, Nixon gave orders for a joint U.S. and ARVN invasion of Cambodia. In April, 30,000 U.S. and 50,000 ARVN troops swept into Cambodia, driving the Vietnamese back and destroying much of the NVA base system. Despite this military success, Congress, reacting to the invasion of a neutral country, passed a measure forbidding the use of U.S. ground troops in Cambodia and Laos.

"We prevented the fall of Cambodia ... undercut North Vietnam's offensive striking power and thereby bought time to press forward with Vietnamization. Our Cambodian incursion was the most successful military operation of the entire Vietnam War."

Richard Nixon defends his illegal invasion in his book, *No More Vietnams*, 1985

INVADING LAOS

After the Cambodian invasion, the North Vietnamese relied more on their bases in Laos, which General Abrams planned to attack in 1971. Because Congress had made it illegal to use American ground troops, the invasion of Laos would be left to the South Vietnamese ARVN. This made it a test of the success of Vietnamization. Could the South Vietnamese defeat the communists on their own?

FULL RETREAT!

On February 8, 21,000 ARVN troops advanced into Laos, where they found 36,000 NVA, equipped with new Soviet tanks, waiting for them. After fierce fighting, the South Vietnamese retreated. They lost half their men, and the survivors only got back thanks to U.S. air support. *Life* magazine published photos of terrified South Vietnamese troops in full retreat as an NVA counterattack defeated the ARVN.

"The NVA drove the invading forces out of Laos with their tail between their legs ... Troops desperate to escape mobbed many of the rescuing helicopters, forcing crewmen to throw them off bodily."

John Saar, "An Ignominious and Disorderly Retreat," *Life* magazine, April 2, 1971

South Vietnamese forces gather before invading Laos.

PEACE WITH HONOR?

In trying to achieve "peace with honor", Nixon's biggest problem was getting North Vietnam to agree to leave the southern government in power. One way of putting pressure on Hanoi was by escalating the air war, with the bombing of Cambodia and North Vietnam. Another was to improve U.S. relations with China and the Soviet Union. Nixon also used what he called a "madman" approach—an attempt to scare the communists into believing that he would use nuclear weapons.

Henry Cabot Lodge, who had been U.S. ambassador to South Vietnam, was head of the American delegation at the Paris talks.

In Paris, between 1969 and 1971, Kissinger had twelve secret meetings with the North Vietnamese negotiators.

PARIS TALKS

In January 1969, peace talks began in Paris between the U.S., North Vietnam, South Vietnam, and the National Liberation Front. Alongside the public talks, there were also secret meetings between the North Vietnamese and Henry Kissinger, Nixon's national security advisor. No progress was made. Hanoi insisted on the complete withdrawal of U.S. troops and the removal of President Thieu's government.

THE MADMAN THEORY

Nixon hoped to use his reputation as a hardline anti-communist to scare the North Vietnamese. "I call it the **madman theory**," he told an aide. "I want the North Vietnamese to believe that I've reached the point that I might do anything to stop the war. We'll just slip the word to them that for God's sake, you know Nixon is obsessed about communism. We can't restrain him when he's angry, and he has his hand on the nuclear button, and Ho Chi Minh himself will be in Paris in two days begging for peace."

As part of his madman tactic, in October 1969 Nixon sent 18 B-52s armed with nuclear weapons to fly toward the Soviet Union.

SILENT MAJORITY

Nixon believed that the antiwar movement damaged his attempts to get Hanoi to negotiate. On November 3, 1969, he made a television address in which he appealed for backing from the "silent majority." He concluded, 'The more divided we are at home, the less likely the enemy is to negotiate ... North Vietnam cannot defeat or humiliate the United States. Only Americans can do that."

Nixon makes his "Silent Majority" speech in 1969.

NIXON IN CHINA

As a way of putting pressure on Hanoi, Nixon improved relations with China, which he visited in 1972. Big divisions had appeared between the Chinese and the Soviets, and Chairman Mao saw the U.S. as a possible ally. At the same time, Nixon also improved relations with the USSR, whose leaders were worried about his visit to China.

Nixon's meeting with Chairman Mao in China alarmed the North Vietnamese, who depended on Chinese military aid.

PEACE TALKS

OPERATION LINEBACKER

Nixon's response to the Easter offensive was his biggest bombing campaign yet. It was aimed at both the invading NVA and the cities of North Vietnam. The campaign, called Operation Linebacker, used hundreds of bombers and fighter-bombers that flew in from U.S. bases in Thailand, Guam, and the Philippines. Nixon told Henry Kissinger, "We will bomb the living bejeezus out of North Vietnam and then if anybody interferes we will threaten the nuclear weapons."

Nixon hoped that his visit to China would lead Hanoi to negotiate. Instead, during Easter 1972, North Vietnam launched a massive new offensive, sending 200,000 NVA troops into South Vietnam. Giap gambled on success because so many U.S. ground troops had been withdrawn.

F-4 Phantom fighter-bombers, flying from Thailand, bomb North Vietnam during Operation Linebacker.

Both Nixon and his security advisor, Henry Kissinger, were secretive men who believed that foreign policy was too complex for the public to understand.

Nixon: I'd rather use the nuclear bomb. Have you got that ready?
Kissinger: That, I think, would just be too much.
Nixon: A nuclear bomb, does that bother you?... I just want you to think big, Henry, for Christ's sake!

Oval Office tape recording, April 25, 1972

An aerial photo shows the damage done by American bombings on Hanoi.

CHRISTMAS BOMBING

In December, due to Thieu's opposition, the peace talks broke down. To reassure Thieu that the U.S. would continue to protect South Vietnam, and to bring the communists back to the talks, Nixon launched Operation Linebacker II. From December 18-30, U.S. B-52 bombers dropped 20,000 tons (18,140T) of bombs on Hanoi and Haiphong.

Vietnamese civilians carry victims of Nixon's Christmas bombing, the heaviest aerial bombardment of the whole war.

OCTOBER AGREEMENT

The bombing campaign and hard fighting by elite ARVN divisions stopped the Easter Offensive and cost the lives of 100,000 NVA troops. For the first time, the North Vietnamese were willing to negotiate. Henry Kissinger and the North Vietnamese politician Le Duc Tho met in Paris where, in October 1973, they reached an agreement. President Thieu would stay in power in Saigon, but the North could keep its troops in South Vietnam. The problem was getting President Thieu to accept this compromize.

"If you accept this agreement, this means you accept to sell South Vietnam to the North Vietnamese communists. As for me, if I accept this agreement, I will be a traitor and seller of the South Vietnamese people."

President Thieu to Henry Kissinger

Kissinger shakes hands with Le Duc Tho, after agreeing on the terms that ended U.S. involvement in Vietnam.

PEACE SIGNED

After the Christmas bombing, the talks started again. At last, on January 27, 1973, Kissinger and Le Duc Tho signed the Paris Peace Accords. Thieu also signed, after the Americans threatened to go ahead without him. Afterward, Kissinger and Le Duc Tho were each awarded the Nobel Peace Prize. Tho refused the award, saying the accords did not guarantee a lasting peace. He was soon proved right.

The Nobel Peace Prize

COMMUNIST VICTORY

THE HO CHI MINH OFFENSIVE

In March 1975, the NVA launched the Ho Chi Minh offensive, its final invasion of South Vietnam. The ARVN fought back, but without U.S. air support and supplies, it could not win. In a lightning campaign, the NVA swept through the south, reaching Saigon in April.

"Units could not move due to lack of gas; artillery could not fire due to lack of shells; modern weapons systems remained unused due to shortages at all levels. Abandoned, the ARVN would fall to ultimate defeat."

Lt General Lam Quang Thi of the ARVN

On March 29, 1973, the last remaining U.S. combat troops left Vietnam. The survival of President Thieu's government depended on continuing U.S. military and financial aid. In 1974, when Congress cut off the aid, South Vietnam was doomed. In December 1974, Pham Van Dong, prime minister of North Vietnam, predicted, "The Americans will not come back even if you offered them candy."

NIXON RESIGNS

In August 1974, Vice President Gerald Ford became president. He replaced Nixon, who had been forced to resign in disgrace following the Watergate political scandal, an effort to subvert the Democratic Party. With Nixon gone, South Vietnam had lost its most powerful defender.

In a long, tearful resignation speech, Thieu accused the Americans of betraying South Vietnam.

President Ford, like most Americans, wanted to move on from Vietnam.

"The Americans have asked us to do an impossible thing ... you have asked us to do something you failed to do with half a million powerful troops and skilled commanders and with nearly $300 billion in expenditures over six long years."

Nguyen Van Thieu resigns as President of South Vietnam, April 21, 1975.

THE FALL OF SAIGON

On April 29–30, with Saigon under attack, U.S. helicopters, flying from carriers, evacuated more than 1,000 Americans and 7,000 Vietnamese from the city. On April 30, NVA tanks smashed their way into the Presidential Palace. In the palace, Colonel Bui Tin of the NVA met General Duong Van Minh, who had replaced Thieu as president. Minh said, "I have been waiting since early morning to transfer power to you." Tin replied, "Your power has crumbled. You cannot give up what you do not have."

Fleeing Americans board a U.S. Marine helicopter in Saigon.

"A WAR THAT IS FINISHED"

On April 23, 1975, shortly before Saigon fell, President Ford said, "Today, America can regain the sense of the pride that existed before Vietnam. But it cannot be achieved by refighting a war that is finished, as far as America is concerned."

NVA soldiers on a Soviet T56 tank force their way into the Presidential Palace.

On a Saigon apartment rooftop, evacuees struggle to find a place on a U.S. helicopter.

AFTERMATH: VIETNAM

WAR WITH CAMBODIA

The unification of Vietnam did not bring peace. In 1975, a new war broke out between Vietnam and the Cambodian Khmer Rouge, backed by China. In 1978, the Vietnamese invaded Cambodia, removing the Khmer Rouge from power. The Chinese then invaded Vietnam, but were driven back. The Vietnamese occupied Cambodia for twenty years.

Troops fight in the Vietnam-Cambodia war, 1979.

Vietnam was now united, but the country had been devastated by the war. Deep divisions remained. Hundreds of thousands of anti-communists were sent to re-education camps, and 60,000 "undesirables" were executed. Communism was imposed as the southern economy was brought under state control.

"Yes, we defeated the United States. But now we are plagued by problems. We do not have enough to eat. We are a poor, underdeveloped nation ... Waging a war is simple, but running a country is very difficult."

Premier Pham Van Dong, 1981

Following the war 1.5 million Vietnamese fled the country by sea. A million of these "**boat people**" became residents of the United States.

An estimated 50,000 children were born to American soldiers and Vietnamese mothers. They were often treated as outcasts in Vietnam.

AGENT ORANGE

The war had a devastating environmental impact. The U.S. Air Force had sprayed vast quantities of Agent Orange, a defoliant, on the Vietnamese countryside. According to the Vietnamese Red Cross, a million Vietnamese have been affected by Agent Orange, including 150,000 children suffering from horrific birth defects.

Planes spray Agent Orange over Vietnam.

THE FALL OF COMMUNISM

The 1991 collapse of communism in the Soviet Union ended already reduced Soviet aid to Vietnam. The government introduced a freer market, and relations with the U.S. improved. In 1994, President Clinton lifted the ban on trade with Vietnam. In 2000, he made the first U.S. presidential visit to the country.

Vietnam is now a tourist destination, and the tunnels where the Viet Cong once hid are now open to visitors, many of them Americans.

Tourists look at a U.S. plane on display in Hanoi's Army Museum.

"Today I am announcing the normalization of diplomatic relationships with Vietnam ... Whatever divided us before let us consign to the past."

President Clinton, July 11, 1995

AFTERMATH: UNITED STATES

The Vietnam War caused deep divisions in the U.S., especially for the generation that lived through the war. There are still arguments about what went wrong. What everybody agreed was that the U.S. had to avoid "another Vietnam." In a 1980 speech to veterans, U.S. President Ronald Reagan claimed that this had led to a "Vietnam Syndrome," which weakened the American will to stand up to aggression.

VIETNAM VETERANS

Unlike the veterans of previous wars, those who returned from Vietnam were not given a hero's welcome. They were seen as losers or blamed for fighting in an unjust war. According to a 1988 survey, 10 percent of those who served suffered from post-traumatic stress disorder, whose symptoms include panic, rage, anxiety, and depression. They suffered from high rates of divorce, suicide, and addiction to drugs and alcohol. One veteran said, "I feel like so much of me died in Vietnam that at times I wished all of me had died over there."

"On returning from Vietnam, minus my right arm, I was accosted twice by individuals who inquired, 'Where did you lose your arm? Vietnam?' I replied, 'Yes.' The response was, 'Good. Serves you right.'"

James W. Wagenbach, Vietnam veteran

The Vietnam War Memorial in Washington is a black marble wall inscribed with the names of 56,000 Americans who died in the war.

Beside the wall, there is a sculpture of three soldiers, who are shown looking in solemn tribute at the names of the fallen.

FILMS AND BOOKS

The Vietnam War has been the subject of many movies, including *Apocalypse Now*, *Platoon*, *Hamburger Hill*, *We Were Soldiers*, *Full Metal Jacket*, as well as books such as Vietnamese writer Bao Ninh's *The Sorrow of War*, which is an international bestseller. Most focus on the traumatic experience of the war for soldiers.

THE POWELL DOCTRINE

In 1990, General Colin Powell drew up a list of conditions to be met before the U.S. went to war again. There had to be a threat to U.S. security, a clearly defined objective, an exit strategy, and wide public and international support. Force should only be used as a last resort. The 1990–1 Gulf War, which aimed to drive Saddam Hussein's invading Iraqi army out of Kuwait, matched all the conditions. After the victory, President George H.W. Bush proclaimed, "By God, we've kicked the Vietnam syndrome once and for all!"

THE IRAQ WAR

In 2003, President George W. Bush launched the invasion of Iraq, beginning a war which did not meet the conditions of the Powell Doctrine, and which lasted for nine years. Many people asked, "Is Iraq another Vietnam?"

IN VIETNAM THE WIND DOESN'T BLOW IT SUCKS

BORN TO KiLL

Stanley Kubrick's
FULL METAL JACKET

VINTAGE BAO NINH

THE SORROW OF WAR

Victory in the First Gulf War restored the reputation of the U.S. military. Here, soldiers wave as their convoy moves into Iraq in 1991.

On May 1, 2003, after the toppling of Saddam Hussein, George W. Bush declares "mission accomplished" in the Iraq War. Despite this, U.S. forces would continue fighting in Iraq until 2011.

MISSION ACCOMPLISHED

GLOSSARY

ARVN
Army of South Vietnam, whose official name was the Republic of Vietnam.

Attrition
Gradual wearing down of an enemy.

Boat People
Vietnamese who fled the country after the communist victory in 1975.

Civil Rights
The rights of citizens to political and social freedom and equality.

Cold War
The struggle between the U.S. and the Soviet Union, lasting from 1945 to 1991.

Colonialism
The conquest and rule of weak nations by rich powerful ones.

Congress
U.S. elected assembly that passes laws and votes on the amount of money that the president can spend.

Domino Theory
President Eisenhower's theory that the fall of one country to communism would set off a chain reaction, leading to more countries falling like dominoes.

DRV
Democratic Republic of Vietnam. During the Vietnam War, it referred only to communist North Vietnam.

Fragging
The killing of unpopular U.S. officers by their own men, using fragmentation grenades.

Guerrilla
A soldier who fights in irregular ways, such as ambush, sabotage, and hit-and-run attacks.

Hanging onto the Americans' Belt
Communist tactic of fighting the Americans at close quarters, so they would not be able to use air power.

Ho Chi Minh Trail
Route used by North Vietnam to send soldiers and arms to the war in the south. The trail also ran through neighbouring Laos and Cambodia.

Indochina
The collective name of Cambodia, Laos, and Vietnam.

Khmer Rouge
The Cambodian communist party.

Madman Theory
Nixon's tactic of scaring the North Vietnamese government into thinking that he was capable of anything, even using nuclear weapons.

Main Force
The full-time fighters of the Viet Cong. Others lived as farmers by day and fighters by night.

Napalm
Jellied petroleum which burns fiercely. The U.S. military fired napalm from flamethrowers and dropped it in bombs.

National Guardsmen
U.S. Armed Forces reservists, called out to maintain order during demonstrations and riots.

Nationalism/Nationalists
Patriotic devotion to one's nation.

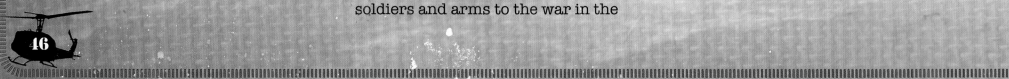

NLF
National Liberation Front. The name of the political wing of the South Vietnamese communist rebels.

NVA
The North Vietnamese Army, the regular troops of the DRV.

PLAF
People's Liberation Armed Forces. The South Vietnamese communist guerrilla army, nicknamed the Viet Cong.

Propaganda
Information spread to promote a political cause or point-of-view.

Referendum
A general vote by the electorate on a single political question.

Rolling Thunder
President Johnson's bombing campaign against North Vietnam, lasting from 1965–8.

Search and Destroy
Large scale U.S. missions to seek out enemy troops and kill as many of them as possible.

Special Forces
Military forces trained for unconventional operations, such as hostage rescue and guerrilla warfare.

Stalemate
State in warfare in which neither side is able to win.

Strategic Hamlets
Fortified villages set up by the U.S. army and ARVN to protect villagers from the Viet Cong.

Tet Offensive
Large scale communist offensive, which took place during the Tet festival in January 1968.

Truman Doctrine
President Truman's belief that it was the U.S.'s duty to help free peoples resist communism anywhere in the world.

Viet Cong
Nickname for South Vietnamese communist guerrillas and members of the NLF.

Viet Minh
League for the Independence of Vietnam, a nationalist organization, led by communists, which fought for independence from French rule.

Vietnamization
U.S. policy to hand over the fighting of the war to the South Vietnamese Army.

This edition published by Scholastic Inc., 557 Broadway, New York, NY 10012

Text, design and illustration © 2014 by Carlton Books Limited. All rights reserved.

Published by Scholastic Inc.

SCHOLASTIC and associated logo are trademarks of Scholastic Inc.

ISBN 978-0-545-79395-7

10 9 8 7 6 5 4 3 2 1

Printed in Hong Kong

Author: Peter Chrisp
Consultant: Dr. Allan R. Millet

Executive Editor: Anna Brett
Design Manager: Emily Clarke
Design: Andy Jones
Illustrations: Peter Liddiard
Picture Research: Steve Behan
Production: Charlotte Cade

47

INDEX

A

Abrams, General Creighton 32, 35
Agent Orange 43
aircraft 15, 20-1, 36, 38, 39
Ali, Muhammad 26
ambushes 22
antiwar movement 26-7, 37
Ap Bia 33
Army of the Republic of Vietnam (ARVN) 11, 16
attrition strategy 16, 21
Australia 3

B

Bao Dai 8, 10-11
boat people 42
bombing 15
Bundy, McGeorge 14, 15
Burma 5
Bush, George H.W. 45
Bush, George W. 45

C

Cambodia 3, 5, 6, 21, 24-5, 34-5, 36, 42
capitalism 4
Chau, Phan Bo 6
China 3, 5, 6, 8, 15, 25, 36-7, 42
civilian casualties 3, 22-3, 29
Clinton, Bill 43
Cold War 3, 4-5
colonialism 6
communism 3, 4-5, 10, 12, 18-19, 42-3
communist victory 40-1
Cronkite, Walter 29, 30
Cu Chi 18

D

Democratic Republic of Vietnam 7, 10
Diem, Ngo Din 10-11, 12-13
Dien Bien Phu 9, 10
Domino theory 5
Dong, Pham Van 40, 42
Duc, Thich Quang 13

E

Easter offensive 38-9
Eisenhower, Dwight D. 5, 11
enclave strategy 16
environmental impact 43

F

Fonda, Jane 27
Ford, Gerald 40-1
fragging 31
French Indochina 5, 6-10

G

Giap, Vo Nguyen 8-9, 20-1, 28, 38
Ginsberg, Allen 26
ground war 16-17
Guam 38

H

Hamburger Hill 33
hanging onto the Americans' belt 21
Hanoi 39
helicopters 20-1
Ho Chi Minh 5, 6-8, 11, 37
Ho Chi Minh offensive 40
Ho Chi Minh trail 18, 24-5
Hue 29

I

Ia Drang 21
Indonesia 5

J

Johnson, Lyndon 13, 14-15, 16-17, 25, 30

K

Kennedy, John F. 12-13
Kent State University 27
Kerry, John 23
Khe Sanh 28
Khmer Republic 34
Khmer Rouge 34, 42
King, Martin Luther 27
Kissinger, Henry 36, 38-9
Korean War 5

L

Laos 3, 5, 6, 21, 24-5, 35
Lenin, Vladimir Ilyich 6
Lodge, Henry Cabot 36
Lon Nol 34-5

M

madman theory 36-7
Main Force 18
Malaysia 5
Mao Zedong 5, 37
McNamara, Robert 14
Minh, General Duong Van 41

N

napalm 21
National Liberation Front (NLF) 11, 19
Navarre, General Henri 9
New Zealand 3
Nguyen Cao Ky 17
Nhu, Madame 13
Nhu, Ngo Dinh 13

Nixon, Richard 33-40
North Korea 4, 5
North Vietnam 7, 10-11, 17
North Vietnamese Army (NVA) 14
nuclear weapons 4, 36-7, 38

O

October Agreement 39
Operation Barrel Roll 25
Operation Linebacker 38-9

P

Paris Peace Accords 39
Paris Peace Talks 36-7
people's courts 22
Philippines 3, 38
Plei Mei 20
Powell Doctrine 45
propaganda 18

R

Reagan, Ronald 44
religious division 10, 13
Rolling Thunder 15
Rusk, Dean 14

S

Saigon 29
   fall 41
Search and Destroy 20-3, 24, 32
Sihanouk, Prince 25, 34
Sihanouk trail 25
silent majority 37
South Korea 3, 4, 5
South Vietnam 3, 7, 10-11, 13, 17
Soviet Union 3-4, 15, 35, 37, 43
strategic hamlets 13

T

Taylor, General Maxwell 14
Tet offensive 28-9, 30
Thailand 3, 5, 38
Thao, Pham Ngoc 13
Thieu, Nguyen Van 17, 37, 39, 40
Tho, Le Duc 39
Tin, Colonel Bui 41
Tonkin Resolution 15
Truman Doctrine 4
tunnel network 18, 22, 43
tunnel rats 22

U

United States 3, 12
   aftermath of the war 44-5
   casualties 3, 15, 21, 33, 44
   draft resisters 26
   entry into war 15, 17
   marines 17
   military advisors 11, 12
   morale 31
   Truman Doctrine 4
   veterans 44

Vietnam Syndrome 44-5
withdrawal 40-1

V

Viet Cong 11, 13, 14, 18-19, 20, 22-3, 28-9
Viet Minh 8-9, 10, 11, 18
Vietnamese unification 42
Vietnamization 32-3, 35

W

Westmoreland, General William 16-17, 20-1, 29, 30
white phosphorus 22
World War II 7

PICTURE CREDITS
The publishers would like to thank the following sources for their kind permission to reproduce the pictures in this book.

Key: t = top, b = bottom, c = center, l = left & r = right

AKG-Images: Getty Images: 7br
Alamy: Editorial: 39br; /Everett Collection Historical: 14t; /US Army Photo: 21l
Bridgeman Images: Private Collection: 15cl
Corbis: Bettmann: 8tr, 11c, 15tc, 20t, 20b, 23tr, 29bl, 35t, 41r; /Tim Page: 29l
Getty Images: AFP: 5tl, 5c, 6c, 7bl, 22bl, 24bl, 25r, 34bl, 37b, 38l, 39tr, 39bc, 40l, 42l; /Alinari: 8l; /Bernie Boston/The Washington Post: 26; /Brodie: 34r; /Larry Burrows/The Life Picture Collection: 3br, 13cl, 13bc, 28t, 35b; /Patrick Christain: 3bl, 21b; /Consolidated News Pictures: 30r; /Eupra/The LIFE Images Collection: 28l; /Fotosearch: 16br; /W.E. Garrett/National Geographic: 42br; /David Greedy: 43tr; /Dirck Halstead: 41t; /Hoang Dinh Nam/AFP: 43br; /Hulton Archive: 1, 21tr; /Stephen Jaffe/AFP: 45tr; /Ken Jarecke/Department Of Defense: 45br; /Keystone-France/Gamma-Keystone: 7b, 37tr, 39tl; /Herve Gloaguen/Gamma-Rapho: 41b; /Jean-Claude Labbe/Gamma-Rapo: 42r; /John Littlewood/The Christian Science Monitor: 27t; /NY Daily News Archive: 12l, 13cr; /Rick Merron/AP Photo: 28b; /Popperfoto: 20bl; /Rolls Press/Popperfoto: 3t; /Co Rentmeester/The LIFE Picture Collection: 32bl; /Howard Ruffner/The LIFE Images Collection: 27b; /Howard Sochurek/The LIFE Picture Collection: 9c; /Sovfoto/UIG: 15cr, 24t, 24-25; /Hank Walker/The LIFE Picture Collection/Getty Images: 5br; /White House Photos: 32-33
Library of Congress: 14bl
Mary Evans Picture Library: Jack Novak: 22tr
National Archives & Records Administration: 16c, 17l, 38r
Postal service of the Bao Dai Government: 8c
Press Association Images: AP Photo: 4c, 9r, 11bl, 11br, 14br, 16tr, 22c, 24c, 27l, 31l. 32r, 33, 36tr, 40r, 43l; /Eddie Adams/AP: 22-23; /Malcolm Browne/AP Photo: 13cl; /CBS/Landov: 29r; /Hoorst Faas/AP Photo: 13tc; /Henry Griffin/AP Photo: 23tl; /Ed Kolenovsky/AP Photo: 26t; /Michel Laurent/AP Photo: 36l; /Nihon Denpa News/AP Photo: 27r
Private Collection: 5tr, 6tr, 7t, 18b, 28c, 30t, 31bl
Rex: Everett Collection: 12r; /Snap: 45l; /Universal Images Group: 31tr
Shutterstock: 44l, 44r
Thinkstock: 4t, 5bl
Topfoto: 9tl, 9bc; /Ullstein Bild: 18t
U.S. Air Force: 34t, 37t
U.S. Department of Defense: 10r, 32c
U.S. Navy: 15b
Courtesy of Vintagebooks.co.uk: 45cl

Every effort has been made to acknowledge correctly and contact the source and/or copyright holder of each picture and Carlton Books Limited apologises for any unintentional errors or omissions, which will be corrected in future editions of this book.

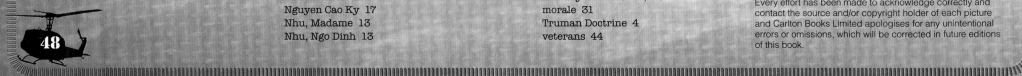